WHEN THE HOLY GHOST SPEAKS, YOU BETTER LISTEN... HEARING THE HOLY SPIRIT

BY: WILLETTE G

GoodwineWPublishing, LLC.
Kingstree, South Carolina

WHEN THE HOLY GHOST SPEAKS, YOU BETTER LISTEN… HEARING THE HOLY SPIRIT

Published by GoodwineWPublishing, LLC.
©2020 Willette G. All Rights Reserved.

No part of this book may be reproduced, distributed, or transmitted in any form, by any means, graphics, electronics, or mechanical (including photocopy, recording, taping, or by any information storage or retrieval system), without written permission from the publisher, except in the case of reprints in the context of reviews, quotes, or references.

Printed in the United States of America
ISBN- 978-1-7331394-6-5

In addition to book signings, Willette G is available for your corporate, conference, church, government agency, non-profit, professional association, and business networking event as a speaker, trainer, or facilitator. Send your requests to goodwinewpublishing@yahoo.com with the subject line *BOOKINGS*.

For more information OR if you are a book club, association, organization, or special interest group, send your inquiries to goodwinewpublishing@yahoo.com (Subject line: *BULK ORDER*). You may also write to: **GoodwineWPublishing, LLC., P.O. Box 592, Kingstree, SC 29556**.

This book contains scriptures from the King James Version of The Holy Bible.

Willette G

RAVE REVIEWS FOR
WHEN THE HOLY GHOST SPEAKS, YOU BETTER LISTEN... HEARING THE HOLY SPIRIT

"I would recommend this book to anyone seeking a new revelation of the Holy Ghost. The author's insight and personal story is relevant to the topic, making it an amazing read. Beautiful!"
- Dr. Inetta Jenkins Fulton

"Yes, yes, yes, the Holy Spirit is, without a doubt, an essential part to living a successful Christian Life. Willette G is certainly correct in pointing out that it is essential to have a prayer life and a connection with JESUS CHRIST in order to even hear the Holy Spirit and be able to benefit from His teachings and guidance, as well as all His other beautiful attributes."
- Robert F. Goodwine, III.

"Willette G is a beautiful & Holy Ghost filled Woman of God. You will truly be blessed by reading this book. I've been waiting for this day. If you're interested in knowing more about the Holy Ghost & its effects on you, then read this book."
- Mary Wyatt Lilliston, Elder
(Joy Church Worship Center, Newport News, VA)

"After reading Chapter 2 and Chapter 3, I was spiritually touched. I was truly convicted to spend more time in God's word. I was also exposed to this material to examine the state of my heart when my personal water baptism took place. This was a time of reflection."

- Angela Garcia, Registered Nurse

DEDICATION

I dedicate this book to the following people:

MY PARENTS

Thank you, my deceased parents, Ola Mae and Robert Goodwine, who always made sure we had. Thank you for always making sure there was a roof over our heads, shoes on our feet and clothes to wear. Thank you for making me do those "Easter Speeches" at church and making me sing in the choir. All that you did and gave has helped shape me into the woman I am today.
Forever grateful.

MY SON

To my one and only son Christopher. I am so blessed to have a young man who loves and serves the Lord. Thank you for living your "Life for Jesus Christ." Thank you for allowing God to use your hands as a musician in the Kingdom. Thank you for standing with me in ministry.

SPECIAL THANKS

To Christina M. Johnson, thank you. Your knowledge, wisdom, expertise, and drive helped push me to the completion of this endeavor.

TABLE OF CONTENTS

DEDICATION ……………………………………....…..9
DON'T QUIT (POEM) ……………………………….…11
INTRODUCTION ……………………………………….13
CHAPTER ONE: WHO IS THE HOLY GHOST? ………..17
REFLECTION QUESTION #1 …………………………..25
CHAPTER TWO: HOW DOES THE HOLY
    GHOST SPEAK? …..………………………………27
REFLECTION QUESTION #2 …………………………....36
CHAPTER THREE: BAPTIZED IN THE HOLY
    GHOST ………………………………………………37
REFLECTION QUESTION #3 ……………………………45
CHAPTER FOUR: DISOBEDIENCE COSTS/
    OBEDIENCE PAYS WELL ……………...………..47
REFLECTION QUESTION #4 ……………………………62
PRAYER …………………………………………….......65
WORKBOOK ……………………………………………69

DON'T QUIT

(POEM ADAPTED BY WILLETTE G; ORIGINAL AUTHOR UNVERIFIED; PUBLIC DOMAIN)

When things go wrong as they sometimes will,

When the road you're trudging seems all up hill,

When the funds are low and the debts are high,

And you want to smile, but you have to sigh,

When care is pressing you down a bit,

Rest if you must, but don't you quit.

Life is strange with it twists and turns,

As every one of us sometimes learns.

And many a failure turns about

When he might have won had he stuck it out.

Don't give up though the pace seems slow,

You might succeed with another blow.

Often the struggler has given up,

When he might have captured the victor's cup. And

he learned too late when the night slipped down,

How close he was to the golden crown.

Success is failure turned inside out,

The silver tint of the clouds of doubt,

And you never can tell how close you are,

It may be near when it seems so far.

So, stick to the fight when you're hardest hit.

It's when things seem worst that you mustn't quit.

INTRODUCTION

Even though it may seem like it, our lives are not our own.

We have a Creator, who is the Almighty God.

We must be obedient to the Creator if we want to spend eternity with Him.

We can't do life however we want to do it, and not pay the consequences of our actions.

There is a guidebook.

It is called the "Bible."

The Holy Ghost helps us to walk that Bible out through Jesus Christ.

We must Listen,

Follow and

Tell others about our soon coming King!

CHAPTER ONE

WHO IS THE HOLY GHOST?

One of the most devastating things, in my opinion, is to have a friend that knows you, cares for you, prays for you, loves you regardless, and most importantly speaks wisdom, knowledge, and truth to you, and YOU DON'T LISTEN.

For the Born-Again Believer we have such a friend available to us, but sometimes we fail to acknowledge Him, trust Him, believe Him, follow His lead, follow His guide, and FAIL TO LISTEN TO HIM.

The person I am speaking of is the "HOLY GHOST."

The Book of Genesis 1:1-2 says, "In the beginning God created the heaven and the earth." Verse 1 is when the Earth is in its first perfect state, which had no sin. Then Lucifer decided that he wanted to seize for himself God's authority over the universe to be worshipped as the Supreme Sovereign of all creation. **HOW CAN THE CREATION TELL THE CREATOR WHAT TO DO?**

So, God cast him out of heaven, and sin begins on the Earth because of Lucifer's rebellion. God allowed the first flood to come upon the Earth to rid it of sin.

Verse 2 says, "And the earth was without form, and void; and darkness was upon the face of the deep. And the Spirit of God moved upon the face of the waters."

So, the "Spirit of God" is the same as the "Holy Ghost." The Spirit of God moved with GOD because He was there in the beginning with God.

In Verse 3, God began to re-create Earth's second perfect state and second habitation. He decided to make man, but man sinned against God. The Earth again became "full of sin," so He spoke to a man named Noah to build an Ark to protect himself, his family, and the animals because a flood was coming, which would rid the earth of sinful men.

After this second flood, God promised that He would never again destroy man by water. As a symbol of His promise he created the "rainbow." And what is so wonderful is that the Holy Ghost was still right there!

Yes, the Holy Ghost, the Spirit of God, and the Holy Spirit are one and the same. I, for a long time, thought they were different. In fact, I even know Bible Scholars to this day who teach that they are not the same.

It is amazing to me that there are churches, in this day and time, that don't teach about the Holy Ghost at all. And if you ask, you may get the response that "we don't teach that here.

As a little girl, I attended a Baptist Church because it was automatic in the house that you went to church. It wasn't an option. We went to church only on the first and third Sundays because those were the "preaching" Sundays. In other words, the Pastor didn't come to church to give a sermon on the second and fourth Sundays.

Mama didn't ask you if you wanted to go to church; it was understood that you were going to church. Not only was it mandatory that you went, but you had to be still and stay awake. At the age of twelve you had to get baptized in water and join the choir. Mama still didn't ask you if you wanted to get baptized or even if you could sing, and you dare not tell her that you didn't want to do either one; that was not allowed.

Sometimes when we went on first and third Sundays and the Pastor would start preaching, there was a tall, slim lady in the back of the church with a white dress, white shoes, and white gloves, who would start saying "Amen." Most people in the church didn't say amen, but she didn't mind. The lady was an usher. And the preaching of the Pastor would sometimes bring such joy to this usher dressed in white that she would move to the aisle and start making this strange movement, with her hands going one way and her feet moving fast. As a child I didn't know what was going on or why this usher was the only one doing this strange movement, but people would say, "Oh, she got the Holy Ghost."

She what? No one else in the whole church "got" the Holy Ghost except this one lady. She was normally incredibly quiet and quite reserved, but when that "Holy Ghost" time would come she wasn't reserved anymore. She would be in the aisle making movements with her hands and feet that were called "shouting." And she was shouting because it was said she had the Holy Ghost. I was frightened because I didn't understand, so I grew up thinking that whenever a person moved their hands and feet like that, they were shouting because they had the Holy Ghost.

I had also heard of the Holy Ghost during baptism. When the Pastor baptized you, he would say "I baptize you in the Name of the Father, the Son and the Holy Ghost." My siblings and I had to attend the after-school program with the Catholic Sisters (known as Nuns) who would also talk about The Father, The Son, and The Holy Ghost, and pray to Mary, the mother of Jesus.

We also gathered around the TV and watched Billy Graham, who would talk about the Holy Ghost.

But the Holy Ghost the usher had gotten didn't seem to be the same Holy Ghost from the baptismal pool, the afterschool program, or the one Billy Graham was talking about.

It is amazing what stays with you from childhood. At the age of 19, while I was serving in the military, a young lady invited me to church. When the music started, the people began acting the same way as the usher had done, and they were speaking a funny language and running around the church. I still had that fear in me from the time I was a little girl. So, when I looked at those people and the way they were behaving I told my friend, "Please don't ever invite me back to this church again."

Little did I know that I *would* end up going back to that church. I enjoyed hanging around this Christian lady because she was so nice, and I knew in order to keep her friendship I would have to go to church. So, I did, even though I wasn't thinking about becoming a Christian. **(We should never allow the unsaved to become so comfortable with us that they look to us instead of looking to Jesus.)** I believed she sensed this about me.

So, one Sunday morning she knocked on the door for me to join her for Church, but when I opened the door, she was dressed in military uniform instead of civilian clothes. She said, "I am not going to church today because I have duty."

So, I said, "If you are not going, then I am not going."

She responded, "The ride is on the way to pick you up so go ahead." And I did.

We got to church, and as I'm listening to the message, although I can't remember the words of the Pastor, I remember thinking that what he said was good and it pricked my heart. But I still had no intentions of getting saved at age 19 because I had already "told" God (ha-ha) that I would get saved at age 25. But that was not God's plan, that was my plan.

All of a sudden, the Pastor asked, "Would anyone like to give their life to Christ today?" People started going up to the front of the church, but I was still sitting and looking. He asked again, "Would anyone else like to give their life to Christ today?"

It's like "something" picked me up and put me in the aisle. I looked at my feet and I was walking up to the front. I looked back at the seat I had been sitting in and I heard a voice in my right ear say, "You don't have to go up there, it is not too late for you to turn around." That was the enemy speaking. And then, I heard a still, small voice say, "Keep going." That was the Holy Spirit. (Many times, we say that " 'Something' told me to call you," or " 'Something' told me not to go that way today." or " 'Something' told me to do this or not to do that," and we fail to recognize that the "Holy Spirit" is speaking.

Well, as I continued walking to the front, people were clapping and happy that I was going up, but I didn't know what was happening to me. When I got to the front the Pastor asked if I wanted to be saved and I said "Yes." He then asked me and the others to repeat after him the verse of Romans 10:9.

Just that quickly, I was "saved." The Pastor asked me for my name, and when I said my last name, *Goodwine*, (because in the military you are called by your last name not your first name) the Pastor said to the congregation, "God has saved the Good Wine for last,." and they gave a little chuckle.

I felt completely different, as if I were a brand-new person. II Corinthians 5:17 says, "Therefore if any man be in Christ, he is a new creature: old things are passed away; behold, all things are become new."

You see, you cannot come to God only when you want to. You can only come to God when the Holy Spirit draws you. John 6:44 says, "No man can come to me, except the Father which hath sent me draw him." I was drawn by the preaching of GOD's Word, and the Holy Spirit convicted me of sin.

That is when it seemed like my heart was pricked. So even after all my years in the church, this Sunday I "heard" the Word and it got in my spirit and it changed my heart. So, when the Pastor gave the invitation for anyone who wanted to give their life to Christ the Holy Spirit drew me.

Hebrews 3:15 says, "Today if ye will hear His voice, harden not your heart." I heard, *didn't harden my heart*, and was able to be drawn, and waiting until age 25, went straight out the window.

About a year later, the military sent me overseas, and I found myself in a church whose congregation was acting the same way as the usher and that church back in the United States. But by this time, I had grown a little bit in the Word of God and now understood what they were doing, because I was now one of those people moving my hands and moving my feet all in the aisles. And I still praise him in the dance, to this very day. Psalms 149:3 says, "Let them praise his name in the dance: let them sing praises unto him with the timbrel and harp."

However, there was still a lot more to learn, because you can praise Him in the dance and still not have the Holy Ghost.

I learned who the Holy Ghost really was and how important it was to have him. He is a person, the third person of the Godhead, sent by both the Father and the Son.

I John 5:7 says, "And there are three who bear witness in heaven: The Father, the Word, and the Holy Ghost and these three are one." You say, "How can three be one?" I often use this analogy, to help people understand this: An egg has a shell, the egg white and the yolk, but it is still one egg. You can separate them and use them in different functions, but it is still "one-egg."

The Father, the Son, and the Holy Ghost are "Three-Yet-One." The "one" means they are one in unity, as well as individually in their roles. The Father does His work, The Son does His Work and the Holy Spirit does His work.

In Luke 2:26-35, The Holy Ghost is again at work. God sends the Angel Gabriel to a virgin by the name of Mary to inform her she had found favor with God.

He also informed her that she would conceive a child in her womb and would call his name Jesus. Mary wondered how this could be possible because of her virginity. The Angel Gabriel told her that the Holy Ghost would come upon her and the power of God would overshadow her, and she would conceive. And it came to pass just as the Angel Gabriel had spoken.

THE HOLY GHOST THAT CAME UPON MARY IS THE SAME SPIRIT OF GOD THAT MOVED UPON THE FACE OF THE WATERS IN GENESIS 1:2.

I Timothy 1:15 tells us that Christ Jesus came into the world to "SAVE SINNERS." He was born to die and His sacrifice and shed blood made it possible for each and every one of us to have a right to the tree of life.

In John 16:7, Jesus speaks to the disciples, saying "Nevertheless I tell you the truth; It is expedient for you that I go away: for if I go not away, the Comforter will not come unto you, but if I depart, I will send him unto you."

The Holy Spirit was sent to save men and anoint them to spread and promote the Gospel.

Jesus was our Comforter while on the Earth, but He did not come to Earth to stay, at that time. So, He tells his disciples, "And I will pray the Father, and He shall give you another Comforter, that he may abide with you for ever." (John 14:16)

REFLECTION QUESTION #1

CAN YOU REMEMBER THE FIRST TIME YOU HEARD OF THE HOLY GHOST OR THE HOLY SPIRIT?

_____
_____
_____
_____
_____
_____
_____
_____
_____
_____
_____
_____
_____
_____
_____
_____
_____
_____

CHAPTER TWO

HOW DOES THE HOLY SPIRIT SPEAK?

Jesus often referred to the Father in carrying out his mission on the earth. In John 12:49, Jesus says, "For I have not spoken of myself, but the Father which sent me, he gave me a commandment, what I should say, and what I should speak."

It is the same with the Holy Spirit. He only speaks what he hears. In John 16:13, Jesus is giving a future revelation of the speaking of the Holy Spirit. That scripture says, "Howbeit when he, the Spirit of truth, is come, he will guide you into all truth: for he shall not speak of himself; but whatsoever he shall hear, that shall he speak: and he will shew you things to come." The truth that the Holy Spirit guides into is the truth about everything wrapped up in Jesus who is the truth, the way, and the life.

It is vitally important that we accept Jesus into our lives, turn our lives over to him, and have a relationship with God. This opens the way for us to hear the Holy Spirit when He speaks. John 8:47 says, "He that is of God heareth God's words: ye therefore hear them not, because ye are not of God."

IF IT CONCERNS YOU, IT CONCERNS GOD. 1 Peter 5:7 says, "Casting all your care upon him; for he careth for you." When we pray in the name of Jesus, because Jesus is our Advocate (1 John 2:1), God hears our every prayer. Then, the Holy Spirit speaks to us what God said concerning us.

When the Holy Ghost speaks, it behooves us to listen. It behooves us to hear Him and walk in obedience because it is coming straight from heaven.

The following are some of the ways the HOLY GHOST speaks:

(1) Comforter - He is called to our side for help or counsel. (John 16:7)

(2) Convincer - He is sent by both the Father and the Son to reprove (tell one's faults, rebuke, convince, convict, expose) the world of sin, and of righteousness, and of judgement. (John 16:8)

(3) Teacher - He shall teach you all things and bring all things back to your remembrance, whatsoever I have said unto you. (John 15:26)

(4) Glorifies Jesus (John 16:14)

(5) Calls and Commissions - Made Us Overseers (Acts 20:28)

(6) He Bears Witness by Anointing Men: In Preaching Luke 4:18; Prophesying Acts 3:21; In the Exercise of Other Gifts (1 Corinthians 12:7-11)

(7) Empowers (I Thessalonians 1:5)

(8) Liberates - Sets Free (Romans 8:2)

(9) Sanctifies - Set Apart (Romans 15:16)

(10) Strengthens (Ephesians 3:16, Acts 1:8)

(11) Helpeth our infirmities: for we know not what we should pray for as we ought: but the Spirit itself maketh intercession for us with groanings which cannot be uttered. (Romans 8:26)

(12) Searcheth the hearts and maketh intercession for the saints according to the will of God. (Romans 8:27)

(13) Gives us power, love, and a sound mind. (II Timothy 1:7)

The Father and the Son sent the Holy Spirit to guide us after Jesus left the Earth.

To have a life of continuously hearing the Holy Ghost and following his lead, we must become familiar with how He speaks to us individually. We need to be filled and baptized in the Holy Ghost. (In Chapter III, I will go more in depth with what that means.)

As we spend more time in prayer, more time in the Word of God, fasting, talking with Jesus, and inclining our ear to his voice, etc., the more we will recognize when the Holy Ghost is speaking.

He also comes in other ways. In the Word of God, he comes as *Fire* (Acts 2:3), as a *Dove* (Luke 3:22), as *Water* (John 7:38), and as *Wind* (Acts 2:2).

We must stay in the Word of God. When the Holy Ghost speaks to us, it triggers from the subconscious mind into the conscious mind.

Have you ever, just all of a sudden, started being concerned about an individual for no apparent reason, and you feel the need to call and see how they are doing? Even if you try and dismiss the thought, it keeps coming back, so, you finally decide to call. When you reach them, you say, " 'Something' told me to call you."

It turns out that the person was going through something and needed a listening ear, or prayer, or help. They were praying to the Lord for help and you called. Your words of encouragement, your prayer, or maybe financial help was what they needed. The Holy Spirit used you to help someone in need. So many times, he comes in that still small voice and what we call "something" is the Holy Ghost speaking.

In my life, the Holy Ghost speaks in certain ways according to what may be happening or is about to happen in my life or someone else's life.

When the Lord wakes me in the morning, the first thing I do before my feet hit the floor is pray and thank Him for waking me. The second thing I do is acknowledge the Holy Spirit. Every morning I say seven times, "I Love You Holy Spirit/Holy Ghost." (I am not saying you have to do that. Yes, the Holy Spirit/Holy Ghost is the same person; I just love saying it that way.) I acknowledge and invite Him into my day, which puts Him in the front of my life so that I can better go about my day.

When you wake up, set your mind on the things of God. If you put a Bible near the bed without having to get up and get one, it makes it so much easier to read and study the Word of God. Command your day by inviting the Father, Son and Holy Ghost in. It will change your perspective and recharge you.

Does that mean that every day I do everything right, or say everything the way it should be said? No, it means I have an Advocate in my Lord and Savior Jesus Christ whose name is above every name, and I can call Him anytime I need Him. And if I do or say anything wrong, I John 1:9 says, "If we confess our sins, He is faithful and just to forgive us our sins, and to cleanse us from all unrighteousness." So, I make sure I repent daily, even if I don't know of anything, I may have done wrong.

If we walk in the flesh and not the spirit then we will go our own way. To walk by the Spirit means I have to walk each moment with the awareness of the Holy Spirit. I must be dependent on Him, sensitive to Him and obedient. If we allow the Holy Spirit to lead, then He will lead us in the right way of doing things, if we LISTEN.

The Holy Ghost will save your life from destruction, keep you from making bad decisions, keep you out of trouble, keep you from messing up your life and someone else's life. He will lead you, guide you, keep you safe, show you the right way and help you to be who GOD has called you to be. He only speaks what He hears.

Here are two instances where the Holy Spirit spoke into my spirit what to say and do. I allowed myself to be led by Him and I take no credit.

On April 4, 2020, around 9:45pm, my phone rang. It was a New York number that I was not familiar with. I was terribly busy, but I felt like I should answer this call. On the other end of the phone was a woman I had met in 2015 who had walked into the church service while I was preaching. After the message I had asked her to introduce herself and she did.

She stated that she was visiting from New York and had come to see her sister, who was extremely ill. She also said that every time she visited her sister, she asked her if she wanted to give her life to Christ. The sister always responded, "Don't come in here talking about God." So, I asked if we could pray for her sister and we did.

After praying, I was led by the Holy Ghost to tell her that when she saw her sister, to ask her again if she wanted to give her life to Christ. She said, "Ok, I will." She wanted my name and phone number and I gave them to her.

A few days later my phone rang, and it was her. She said, "I did as you said. When I asked my sister if she wanted to give her life to Christ, she answered 'YES'! It's like she was waiting for me to come. She did it so easily."

The lady went back to New York, and a few weeks later she called again to tell me the sister had passed.

The Holy Spirit had prepared the sister's heart, and when she came to visit, the Holy Spirit drew her. It was the Holy Spirit speaking through me with instructions for her sister. Zechariah 4:6 says, "Not by might, nor by power, but by my spirit, saith the LORD of hosts."

Five years later, on that evening of April 4, 2020, the lady from New York called again. She began telling me that she had misplaced my number but had found it recently and had placed it on her refrigerator. Every time she walked by that refrigerator, she felt the leading to call me, but didn't know why, so she didn't. She kept feeling she should call, and finally decided to listen.

She began telling me about her brother whom the Spirit had been leading her to check on. When she finally reached him, the brother was sick in the house. She convinced him to go to the hospital and he found out he had pneumonia. She told me she ministered to him, on several occasions, to turn his life over to Jesus. But he wouldn't do it.

I felt the prompting of the Holy Spirit to remind her of the situation with her sister. So, I said to her, "I believe the Holy Spirit wants you to ask your brother again if he would like to give his life to Christ now. So, hang up with me and call him right now, because he is ready." She said "Ok, let me call him right now and I will call you back."

About ten minutes later she called me to tell me she did as I said, and her brother accepted Jesus into his life right there on the phone while in the hospital. HALLELUJAH! PRAISE JESUS!

On April 8, 2020, the hospital decided to put the brother in an induced coma because of the pneumonia. On April 14, 2020, he came out of the coma and was responding to text messages. On April 19, 2020, God called him home.

The Holy Ghost knew because He speaks what He hears. That is why the brother was so heavy on the sister's heart. The Holy Ghost moved on her to agree with someone else concerning her brother's situation and again began speaking through me to her concerning his salvation, just as He did with her sister.

Now, that sister from 2015 and the brother from 2020 are both in Heaven to forever be with the Lord. I say again HALLELUJAH, HALLELUJAH PRAISE JESUS!

As Christians we must be laborers for the Kingdom. We have the power to slow hell from enlarging itself by telling men and women that Jesus loves them and died for all their sins. No matter what those sins are, REPENT, REPENT!

We have to be sensitive to the Holy Spirit because He is constantly speaking to us.

>The Holy Spirit bears witness to our spirit. (Romans 8:16)

REFLECTION QUESTIONS #2

CAN YOU RECALL A TIME WHEN YOU FELT A PROMPTING FROM THE HOLY SPIRIT, IN YOUR SPIRIT OR HEARD A WORD TO DO OR SAY SOMETHING?

_____
_____
_____
_____
_____
_____
_____
_____
_____
_____
_____
_____
_____
_____
_____
_____

CHAPTER THREE

BAPTIZED IN
THE HOLY GHOST

There are three Baptisms for the Believer: First, Baptism into Christ and into His body, followed by Water Baptism and Baptism in the Holy Ghost. (The last two don't have a set order to them .)

Some churches pray for the person to receive the Baptism of the Holy Ghost as soon as they repent of their sins. Some churches schedule a new Child of God immediately as a candidate for Water Baptism. All three play a vital role.

As I previously stated, you cannot come to Jesus unless the Holy Spirit draws you. So, when you are drawn and you repent of your sins, you are Baptized into Jesus Christ or into His body and the new birth. This is the first Baptism because it brings you into the Body of Christ. This is what is meant in Ephesians 4:5: "One Lord, One Faith, One Baptism." That Baptism is not talking about water, it ushers you into the Kingdom. You are now a *Child of God*.

So, this Baptism has to be done first. It comes through repentance and asking Jesus to come into your heart and forgive you of all your sins. This is why you may hear some people say you have the Holy Spirit when you first get saved.

A much-used Scripture that is used to lead people to the Lord is Romans 10:9-10 that says, "That if thou shalt confess with thy mouth the Lord Jesus, and shalt believe in thine heart that God hath raised him from the dead, thou shalt be saved. For with the heart man believeth unto righteousness; and with the mouth confession is made unto salvation."

Please repent, repent, repent, for the Kingdom of Heaven is at hand! WE MUST BE BORN AGAIN.

Either of the next two Baptisms can come next. However, *Water Baptism* and *Baptism in the Holy Ghost* both play a vital role in the life of every believer.

Let's talk about Water Baptism. There is no need to be baptized in water if you have not confessed your sins and given your heart to Jesus. Water Baptism is an outward expression of an inner experience. If you are not born again, you are just getting wet.

In John 1:32-34, Jesus is now ready to be baptized in water. You may be asking why would Jesus, who knew no sin, get baptized? I am glad you asked that question (smile).

There are two reasons why Jesus submitted to Water Baptism:

1) Matt 3:15 says, "And Jesus answering said unto him, 'Suffer it to be so now: for thus it becometh us to fulfill all righteousness.' " The "us" is John the Baptist and Jesus.

He has come to the Jordan River to be baptized and John is saying "I need to be baptized of you, and you're coming to me?" Jesus answered "suffer" or allow this to happen. He said this because they were both sent of God and had to fulfill what they were sent to do.

2) Jesus had to be baptized so that he could be manifested to Israel. John 1:31-32: "And I knew him not: but that he should be made manifest to Israel, therefore am I come baptizing in water. And John bare record, saying, 'I saw the Spirit descending from heaven like a dove, and it abode upon him. And I knew him not: but he that sent me to baptize with water, the same said unto me, upon whom thou shalt see the Spirit descending, and remaining on him, the same is he which baptizeth with the Holy Ghost. And I saw and bare record that this is the Son of God.' "

Jesus the Messiah had to be introduced to Israel. God's plan was to offer salvation first to the Jews before going to the Gentiles.

Matt 3:16-17 beautifully says "And Jesus, when he was baptized, went up straightway out of the water: and, lo the heavens were opened unto him, and he saw the Spirit of God descending like a dove, and lighting upon him. And lo a voice from heaven saying, 'This is my beloved Son, in whom I am well pleased.' " Oh my, my, my just visualizing that makes me want to praise Him. To God Be the Glory!

Water Baptism is a symbol of the death, burial, and resurrection of Jesus Christ. This is demonstrated by being immersed in water. Many churches have a baptismal pool located right in the church; some go to a river and baptize. We show that we are dying to the old and rising anew.

**However, we must remember that
Water Baptism does not save you.
It is a part of the Christian experience.**

In Chapter 1, I talked of how I was baptized at the age of twelve in the Baptist Church. That Baptism was done out of obedience to my parents. Unfortunately, it was not valid because I wasn't a Christian. As sincere as it may have appeared, I was simply going through the motion.

So, when the military gave me orders to go overseas, they routed me to Ft. Benjamin Harrison, Indiana first, so that I could receive training to work in the Post Office when I got to Germany. While in Indiana I visited a church one Sunday. Well, the message happened to be on Water Baptism.

At this time, I didn't know that the baptism done as a child didn't count. The preacher started saying that if you haven't been baptized since you got saved, you had to be baptized. And then he said, "You have to be baptized in the name of Jesus." I had never heard that before, because in the Baptist church it was Father, Son and Holy Ghost. (But that's another book.) So, I was thinking, "Do I really have to do this again?" I didn't want to because, at age 16, I had been thrown into a pool and almost drowned. So, my fear of water was huge.

But when you love the Lord and you want to follow his Word you try to do what He says. Luke 6:48 says "And why call ye me, Lord, Lord and do not the things which I say?" So, when they asked if there were any candidates for baptism, I told the usher I wanted to but didn't have a change of clothes. Well, this church had the clothes for you to put on, so I had no excuse.

Even though I was terrified of water, I changed my clothes and I got in the pool. The preacher started talking and I was thinking he was going to hold my nose, but he didn't! He quickly said, "I baptize you in the Name of Jesus" and dunked me. I wasn't prepared to gather myself and hold my breath, so when they brought me back up, I was choking! I could hear the people saying, "She didn't hold her breath." But they were able to help me get it together. After I got dressed, I said to Jesus, "I only did that because I love you, but please Lord I pray I won't ever have to do that again" (smile). John 14:15 says "If you love me, keep my commandments."

It should be the mission of every believer to want GOD to be so pleased with our lives that He can say, "This is my son, this is my daughter in whom I am well pleased." We should live our lives so that we can hear, "Well done, good and faithful servant. Enter into the joy of thy Lord." (Matthew 25:23)

Now let's talk about being "Baptized in the Holy Ghost."

First and foremost, Jesus is the Giver of the Baptism of the Holy Ghost (Matthew 3:11). Everything we receive, it is still Jesus who gives it. Jesus comes through the Person of the Holy Ghost..

So, we have received the initial Baptism; we have been Baptized by immersion in water, and now we need the Baptism of the Holy Ghost.

The Holy Spirit is promised to all children of God. All children of God are given the Spirit in a measure after the new birth.

Luke 11:13 says "If ye then being evil know how to give good gifts unto your children: how much more shall your heavenly Father give the Holy Spirit to them that ask him?" This asking is for the Holy Spirit after we become the children of God. This asking is to be endued with power from on high. This asking is to be Baptized in the Holy Ghost.

The Book of Luke 1:15, tells us that John the Baptist was filled with the Holy Ghost from his mother's womb. However, this was only a measure. John was not Baptized with the Holy Ghost. In Matt 3:14, when Jesus is coming to be baptized, John says to Him "I have need to be baptized of thee…" John desired the Baptism of the Holy Ghost, but it was not given until Jesus left.

The disciples had been Children of God for years. They had walked with Jesus, talked with Jesus, and seen him do many miracles.

In John Chapter 20, Jesus had risen from the dead and Mary Magdalene came and told the disciples that she had seen the Lord and he had spoken things to her. The disciples had assembled themselves together because they were afraid of the Jews and were hiding. Well, Jesus appeared in the midst of them and said to them, "As my Father hath sent me, even so send I you." And Jesus breathed on the disciples and said "Receive ye the Holy Ghost."

The Holy Ghost that Jesus breathed on them was only a measure. They did not receive the Baptism of the Holy Ghost. In other words, they received a filling, but they didn't have the fullness.

In Luke 24:49, Jesus tells the disciples to "tarry ye in the city of Jerusalem until ye be endued with power from on high." This was to be Baptized in the Holy Ghost with the full enduement of power from on high to do the works of Christ, and to start their ministry.

Acts 5:16: If a Christian is filled, they have a measure and they are limited in spiritual power. If a Christian is Baptized in the Holy Ghost, they have the fullness and there is no limitation. I Corinthians 12:4 & 11 says, "Now there are diversities of gifts, but the same Spirit. But all these worketh that one and the selfsame Spirit, dividing to every man severally as he will." It is the Holy Ghost who gives Spiritual Gifts and divides them. So, a believer can operate in all the gifts, it is according to the gifts the Holy Spirit gives to them.

Acts 1:8: "But ye shall receive power after that the Holy Ghost is come upon you; and ye shall be witnesses unto me both in Jerusalem, and in all Judaea, and in Samaria and unto the uttermost part of the earth."

Acts 2:1-4: "And when the day of Pentecost was fully come, they were all with one accord in one place. And suddenly there came a sound from heaven as of a rushing mighty wind, and it filled all the house where they were sitting. And there appeared unto them cloven tongues like as of fire, and it sat upon each of them. And they were all filled [*meaning they were all filled and baptized*] with the Holy Ghost, and began to speak with other tongues, as the spirit gave them utterance."

It is vitally important to get Baptized in the Holy Ghost. Some teach that if you get Baptized in the Holy Ghost you must speak in Tongues immediately, and some teach as you continue to seek the Lord the evidence of speaking in Tongues will come at another time (that is also another book), but you should speak at some point. It is not always in a church setting that you may be Baptized in the Holy Ghost. You can be Baptized in your home during your prayer time, or while you may be studying, etc. Ask the Lord to Baptize you. Just lift your hands, open your mouth, and begin praising and thanking him. Forget about yourself and concentrate on Him. He said He will give it to you if you ask. Don't be afraid to speak in Tongues. Whether you speak immediately or later, I Corinthians 14:39 says, "Forbid not to speak in tongues."

The Holy Ghost wants to hear your voice, He wants to hear you say something. He will take your words and translate them.

Romans 8:27 says, "And he that searcheth the hearts knoweth what is the mind of the Spirit, because he maketh intercession for the saints according to the will of God."

Acts 2:39: "For the promise is unto you, and to your children, and to all that are afar off, even as many as the Lord our God shall call."

Ephesians 6:18: "Praying always with all prayer and supplication in the Spirit and watching thereunto with all perseverance and supplication for all saints."

REFLECTION QUESTION #3

WHAT DOES IT MEAN TO BE BAPTIZED IN THE HOLY GHOST?

_____
_____
_____
_____
_____
_____
_____
_____
_____
_____
_____
_____
_____
_____
_____
_____
_____
_____

CHAPTER FOUR

DISOBEDIENCE COSTS, OBEDIENCE PAYS WELL

In the next few pages, you will find real-life stories of my life, when I listened to the Holy Ghost and followed His instructions, and things turned out well.

You will also find real-life stories of my life when I did not listen to the Holy Ghost, did not follow His instructions, and things cost me heavily.

You may find some humor in some of the stories, but I pray that this book will enlighten you, cause you to dig deeper in the Word of God, and cause you to walk closer to Him.

The stories are absolutely true, and names have been left out intentionally. I will give a story about Obedience, then a story of Disobedience and back to Obedience, etc. One story in particular I added, so that the "Single Ladies" can take some notes. I have many experiences to write about, so these are just a few.

God's many blessings upon you as you read them and if any of them can stop you from making some of the mistakes I made, then PRAISE JESUS. And if some of them can cause you to walk in the power and authority that the Christian has then I say to GOD Be the Glory and PRAISE JESUS.

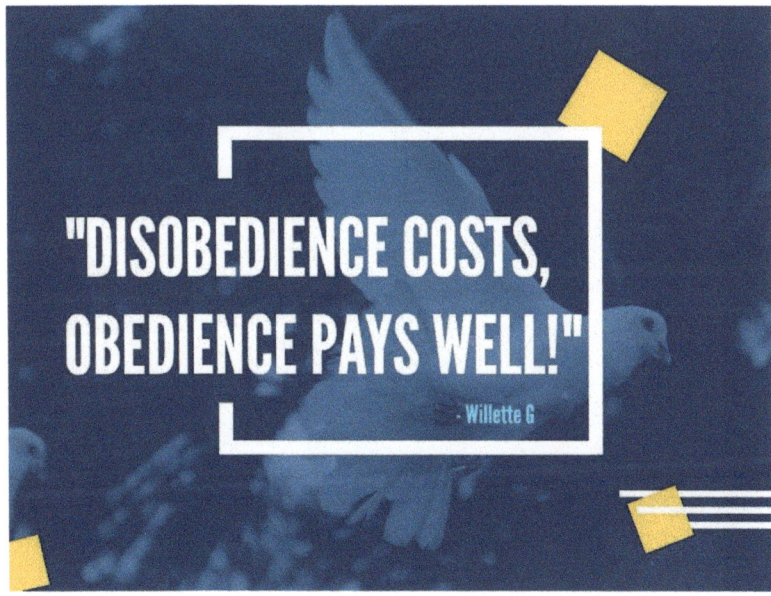

OBEDIENCE PAYS WELL

"WHO LEFT THE DOG OUT?"

I own rental properties, and part of owning rentals is keeping up with the maintenance, inspections, etc. It was now time for an annual inspection at one of the properties. So, I contacted the residents, and sent them a written notice stating the date and time I would be there. The residents replied by phone stating they would not be home but agreed that I could go ahead with the annual inspection in their absence. They also stated, "We will have the dog in its kennel, so you're free to check all of the property."

I arrived as agreed. The back of the property has a chain-link fence which starts at the back of the house, so I decided to walk around the back yard first. I opened the gate, closed the gate back and started to walk in the yard. As I turned around, I saw this big, husky, wolf-looking dog galloping towards me like a horse. I had no time to open the gate and get out, and no time to run or get out of the path of this humongous animal. I just knew I was about to be attacked, and all of a sudden, I heard a voice say, "START SINGING."

There may be times in your life when the Holy Ghost will speak to you and you will need to respond quickly. You won't have time to debate about it, or try to rationalize what He just said, or think, "Should I do this or not?" JUST DO IT!

I started singing "Amazing Grace." I don't know why I chose "Amazing Grace"; it just came out without thinking about it. As I sang, that galloping, looking horse started slowing down and by the time he got to me it was like he became a little puppy. I was standing in the yard rubbing the dog's head and singing to him, and he looked at me as if I were singing like an angel. If I didn't know Jesus was real, I found out that day!

The interesting part is while I was singing and rubbing this dog's head, the back door opened, and the couple stepped out. I looked at them like, "You are not supposed to be home." They said," Oh he must like you." What? Like me? And then they said, "We found out we could be here, and we forgot to call you and tell you." So, they called the dog and put him back in the kennel.

"PRAISE JESUS!

HE BLESSED ME WITH A VOICE TO SING."

DISOBEDIENCE COSTS

"THE DRIVE HOME"

Sometimes, when there is danger concerning myself or a family member, I get this awful ache in the pit of my stomach. It is different from a regular tummy ache. And I know the difference. This is when the Holy Ghost is letting me know there is danger ahead.

I work in a different city than I live in. On this particular evening, that awful ache came, and I heard that still, small voice say, "Don't drive home this evening. Stay in the city." But I began to rationalize saying to myself, "It won't take me long to get home. If I leave now, I should be fine." <u>Simple Disobedience.</u> The enemy had it set for me to die that evening. But I am a praying woman and even though I heard the Holy Spirit, I felt I could turn that thing around. So, I prayed "Lord protect me on these dangerous highways. Let no hurt, harm or danger come nigh me in Jesus name.."

I have traveled this same route for years, so I am confident, because I am familiar with the route and never had a problem. But when you don't listen, disobedience will cost you.

The trip was going well, until I got about twenty minutes from my home, and I kid you not, all of a sudden, I looked to the left and I saw something huge with horns coming into my driver's door. This thing was headed straight into me. And I immediately said, "Oh no, devil, I am not dying tonight." I put the pedal to the metal. When I got to the next station I pulled over. My car was damaged on the driver's side, but the door didn't even have a scratch. I was thinking, "Was that a buck that just hit my car?" I don't know to this day for sure, because I went back the next morning when it was light outside and saw not one trace of a deer or any animal.

I called my insurance company and when they were through inspecting the car, it came to over $6,000.00 in damages, but not one strand of hair on my head had been touched. I was not hurt at all. When I saw my car, I couldn't believe that in that short span of time that much damage could have been done.

When you have been Baptized in the Holy Ghost you have been endued with power from on high. I believe that, even though I was disobedient, when I said that prayer before getting on the road the Lord honored it and I was not killed! WHEN THE HOLY GHOST SPEAKS YOU BETTER LISTEN!

OBEDIENCE PAYS WELL

"THE REFRIGERATOR"

It has been quite a few years, but I will never forget this particular time when my mother lived not far from me. I could get to her place in about seven minutes.

So, this particular day, I had scheduled myself to do nothing but my housework. I started cleaning and I am just cleaning away, got the music playing and I am just singing and cleaning. (I sing for breakfast, lunch, and dinner (smile).)

In the middle of cleaning, the Holy Spirit says, "Go clean your mother's refrigerator." I said, "What, go clean the refrigerator, clean the *Refrigerator*?" I said, "Now Lord, how am I going to call my mother and tell her I am coming over to clean her refrigerator? She is going to be insulted." He spoke again, "Go clean your mother's refrigerator."

There are times when the Holy Ghost will speak things for you to do that just don't add up to you. But the Word of God says, "For my thoughts are not your thoughts, neither are your ways my ways, saith the Lord." (Isaiah 55:8)

Well, out of obedience, I picked up the telephone and called my mother. I had to *swallow for a minute* because I didn't know how to present this task. So, I asked her how she was doing, and if she was busy. She said "No," so I said, "Would you mind if I came over and cleaned your refrigerator?" She said, "Come and clean my refrigerator? You might need to clean your own refrigerator." Yes, she was insulted. But I knew the Holy Spirit had spoken and regardless of my mother's response, I knew I had to go. I was compelled to go, whether I wanted to or not.

So, I just listened as she "kinda" told me off. And when she finished, I said "I'll be over there in a few minutes." When I got there my mother gave me "that look." My mother had a way of looking at you that would cause you to straighten up and fly right.

She only had to spank me one time in my whole life. That look would do it. But let me give you a little humor and veer off for just a moment, to tell you about my one spanking.

I was about 6 years old and Mother would always dress us nicely with the lace socks, clothes always matching, hair done, clothes pressed. We went to school looking genuinely nice.

This particular morning, she had a dress out for me to wear that I did not like. But during that time, you could not tell your mother what you were or weren't going to wear.

I didn't like this dress because it made me look fat and I would get teased and called "Piggly Wiggly." Also, there were two boys in my class whose chairs were assigned at the same table I was. When you wore a dress and the teacher wasn't looking, they would feel your legs under the table. So, I was determined I was not going to be teased on this day and those boys wouldn't get the chance to feel my legs.

My sisters and I would walk to school, and mother would stand on the porch until we got around a certain curve and she would go back in the house. This time, I walked around the curve and stopped. I waited a few minutes when I thought she was probably back in the house and I turned around.

Right next to our house was the Holiness Church. I knew I couldn't go back home, and I wasn't going to school. So, I walked on the far side of the Holiness Church, away from the side of our house, so I could get to the back steps. I sat down on those steps the entire day. I was hiding behind the Church (and that is another book).

What I didn't realize was that from the kitchen window my mother could see behind the church. She let me sit there all day and never said a word.

When I thought school was out, I walked into the yard as if I were just getting home from school. She asked me, "Did you go to school today?" I answered, "Yes."

My mother put a "whippin" on me that still lasts until this very day. I never needed another and I never had to wear that dress again.

DON'T HIDE BEHIND THE CHURCH.

Ok, back to the refrigerator. I walked in and as I said she gave me that look, and I just played it off. I felt so awkward, but I went into the kitchen and started cleaning the refrigerator and singing.

After being there for about twenty minutes, I heard a loud noise, and said, "Mama, what was that?" I didn't hear her say anything, so I walked into the living room area where she was sitting.

Just that quick my mother had fallen and was on the floor having a heart attack. I called 911 and they got there in a hurry. They put her in the ambulance and took her to the hospital where she stayed for a few days and was released to come home.

God knows all things. He knows our end from the beginning. Had I not listened to the Holy Ghost speaking and followed His instructions, the outcome may have been quite different.

Sometimes God's assigned tasks seem as if He has chosen the wrong person or given you the wrong assignment. He never makes a mistake. He is a perfect God. He is the Almighty. If God put it to your hands to do, you can do it with the help of the Holy Ghost.

DISOBEDIENCE COSTS

(THIS IS MAINLY FOR THE SINGLE LADIES)

"PAY ATTENTION"

I was in my forties and had worked ever since I was a teenager. And at this time my insurance company wanted me to put a new roof on one of my properties. I heard of a company that was looking for people with college degrees to grade college students' papers. That sounded like a good idea to help pay for the roof. They paid very well. So, after my regular job, I would go grade papers.

Well, at my main job I had a huge office with a nice big window, and often I would see this gentleman come by and just look at me and wave. So, one day he got bold enough to come into the office and introduce himself. He was an older gentleman who had retired and worked out all the time. He did not look his age. It turns out he was in his sixties.

He kept coming back, but I wasn't really interested because he was a little old for me. My supervisor and all the people on the job convinced me what a nice man he was, and he was looking for a wife and to just give the man a chance.

I decided to invite him to church and introduced him to the Pastor. He was a church-going man, well dressed, fancy car, nice house, and seemed well-to-do, But I have never been interested in a man for his material possessions. How is your heart?

(Ladies, always invite him to your church and see how he flows. And always visit his church: (1) Once without him not knowing that you're coming and (1) With him and see how he flows. It will tell you a whole lot. If he won't take you to his church, it's a red flag. Pay attention.)

At that time, I was one of the ordained ministers in the congregation and regularly active in the church. I was on the Praise Team, Choir, and Leader of the Weekly Bulletin Ministry and Preaching. I wanted him to see who he was pursuing. I also made it clear that if he were interested in me and seriously interested in marriage, there would be no "booty call" before marriage. He wholeheartedly agreed.

One day while working at my main job he called me and asked if I would come over for lunch. He loved to cook. I said, "Sure."

When I arrived, he had everything prepared as I sat down to feast. While eating he handed me a white envelope, and I asked, "What is this?" I opened the envelope and it was a "Certified Check" with my name on it for $8,000. (Not $80, not $800, but $8,000!) I couldn't eat after that.

Now as I stated earlier, I have worked since I was 16 years old and raised to be independent. My mother taught us that if you want something you work for it. That is why I had the other paper grading job to repair the roof. I wasn't accustomed to a man giving me money. So, I looked at that check, and I looked at him. He said "I don't like you having to work two jobs. Take this money and repair the roof on your house. Since we are going to be getting married, I am giving you this.

I looked at him again and I asked, "Is this money I am going to have to pay back?" He said "No." I put the check in my pocketbook. I would take it out and look at it and put it back and take it out and look at it over and over. And something just didn't feel right about that check. This went on for days.

But this particular day I had to go shopping for the company because budgeting and spending was a part of my job. I got to the place where I normally shopped, stepped out of my car, and in front of my feet were two crisp $50 bills. I looked around to see if someone had just dropped them. I saw a man walking by and I asked, "Sir, did you just drop any money?" and he responded "No."

I picked up the two $50 bills and I heard a voice say, "I WILL PROVIDE FOR YOU." I knew that was the Holy Spirit speaking and that meant to give the man that $8,000 check back. God had shown up and showed me how quickly he could supply my need.

I have never been a lover of money, but my flesh, my eyes, looked at that $8,000 check one too many times. I decided to sign my name on the back and went to the bank, in spite of what I had heard from the Holy Spirit.

I John 2:16 says "For all that is in the world, the lust of the flesh, and the lust of the eyes, and the pride of life, is not of the Father, but is of the world."

I took the $8,000 and I hired contractors to repair the roof. Once the roof had been repaired and I had paid everyone, the man asked, "Have you cashed the check yet?" He knew the answer before he even asked, because this was the first time he asked about it since giving it to me. He waited until it had cleared.

I said, "Yes, I have already paid all the contractors." He said, "I thought about it after I gave you that money and I shouldn't have done that." I said, "Well the money has been spent on the contractors and material." So, he said to me, "IF YOU HAVE SEX WITH ME, I WILL FORGET ABOUT THE MONEY." I said, "Forget about the money. I don't owe you any money. You said it was a gift." I couldn't believe he said that!

The HOLY SPIRIT had spoken to me through the two $50 bills and told me I WILL PROVIDE FOR YOU and I didn't listen. It was a set-up. It was a trick of the enemy to interfere with my walk with the Lord. It broke my heart, but what he didn't know was that I love the Lord more than I loved anybody. And I said to him, "How dare you agree to a relationship of abstinence and change courses in the middle of the stream?" He told me either I have sex, or give him the $8000 back, or he would take me to court.

I walked away speechless. He began harassing me, threatening me, coming to my job and telling everyone I took his money, went to my supervisor and told him I took his money, went to the church and tried to discredit me and make me look bad. He would come into my office and tell me, "All you have to do is give in." I still wouldn't say anything to him. And it angered him. He said, "I will die and go to hell before I let a woman take my money and I don't get any _____." (You can fill in the blank.)

I had to go in my secret closet because I was beginning to get angry and the Word of God said in Ephesians 4:26, "Be angry but sin not." I knew if I got angry with him, I would sin. So, I stayed before the Lord because I knew I was going through this experience because of my disobedience.

After he saw that I was not giving in no matter what he said or did, he filed court papers against me. I had to answer the court papers and explain the situation. I explained to the courts that I was being sexually harassed and was being asked for money I didn't owe. I was sent a date to appear in court.

Well, I just knew that this case was going to be thrown out, so I did not get a lawyer. He came in with a lawyer and when the Judge heard my side, He said, "I believe you, but the fact remains you did receive the money."

I said, "Yes, I received it, but I didn't ask for it. It was a gift." And even though the judge said he believed my side of the story, he ruled in his favor.

Not only did he order me to pay him $8,000 but I had to pay court costs and interest. I, for the first time in my life had a judgment against me, with my name on it. That does not go well with being in ministry. I could not believe it! I have yet to this day to ever speak a word to that man because I know God has a way when people do you wrong. Romans 12:19 says, "Vengeance is mine; I will repay, saith the Lord."

With the help of the Good Lord I paid him back $8,000 and court costs. They threw out the interest. PRAISE JESUS!

This is for anybody, but I especially speak to the ladies. Keep yourself for the right person that God has for you. I had to learn to let the Holy Ghost dwell in me so that my body would be a vessel of honor before the Lord. Don't give your pearls to the swine, especially for money. God is big enough to supply your need. The cattle on a thousand hills belong to Him. Ladies you are not a piece of meat, for someone to try out to see..... . GOD IS GREATER!

Any man who tells you that if you don't give your body to him, he will not marry you, wipe the dust off your feet and keep it moving. He is not ready for a Godly woman. And you do not have to settle. GOD has someone who will see how special you are, and he will be a real man of GOD. Not someone who just goes to church on Sunday. Not enough of this is taught in the Body of Christ and all kinds of things are going on in the church house.

JESUS IS SOON TO COME! This Coronavirus was allowed for a reason. However, according to II Chronicles 7:14, "If my people which are called by my name, shall humble themselves, and pray, and seek my face, and turn from their wicked ways, then will I hear from heaven, and will forgive their sin, and will heal their land."

LET US ALL REPENT AND PREPARE TO MEET OUR SOON COMING KING!

REFLECTION QUESTION #4

(A) THINK OF A TIME WHEN YOU WERE DISOBEDIENT TO THE LEADING OF THE HOLY GHOST AND IT COST YOU.

_____
_____
_____
_____
_____
_____
_____
_____
_____
_____
_____
_____
_____
_____
_____
_____
_____

(B) THINK OF A TIME WHEN YOU WERE OBEDIENT TO THE LEADING OF THE HOLY GHOST AND IT PAID WELL.

_____
_____
_____
_____
_____
_____
_____
_____
_____
_____
_____
_____
_____
_____
_____
_____
_____
_____
_____
_____
_____
_____
_____
_____

PRAYER

FATHER,

IN THE NAME OF JESUS, I THANK YOU FOR ALLOWING ME TO WRITE THIS BOOK. LET IT TOUCH THE HEARTS AND MINDS OF EVERYONE WHO MAY READ IT.

HOLY GHOST/HOLY SPIRIT, HAVE YOUR WAY

AMEN, AMEN, AMEN.

WORKBOOK

I Pray you have been enlightened by this book and will take the time to further dig into the Word of God. I also pray you allow His Word to become the most important thing in your life.

Be sure to answer all of the Reflection Questions at the end of each chapter and allow them to bring you closer to Him.

THE BOOK OF JUDE VERSES 20-23 GIVES SEVEN CHRISTIAN PRACTICES THAT GUARANTEE SECURITY. IT INCLUDES THE HOLY GHOST, SO I THOUGHT IT WOULD MAKE A GOOD SPIRITUAL EXERCISE FOR YOU TO STUDY.

The Seven Commands will enhance your daily walk with the Lord. Take your time and study them, write your thoughts, increase your knowledge, and watch God move in your life as you apply them.

God's Many Blessings and May Heaven Smile Upon You.

Thank you for investing in the Kingdom.

ROMANS 14:17: FOR THE KINGDOM OF GOD IS NOT MEAT AND DRINK, BUT RIGHTEOUSNESS, AND PEACE, AND JOY IN THE HOLY GHOST

WILLETTE G

FIRST COMMAND:
BUILD UP YOURSELVES ON YOUR MOST HOLY FAITH
(V.20 / I TIMOTHY 1:4)

SECOND COMMAND:
PRAY IN THE HOLY GHOST
(V. 20; EPHESIANS 6:18; ROMANS 8:26)

THIRD COMMAND:
KEEP YOURSELVES IN THE
LOVE OF GOD
(V. 20; II TIMOTHY 1:14; ROMANS 8:35-39)

FOURTH COMMAND:
LOOK FOR THE MERCY OF OUR LORD JESUS CHRIST
(V. 21; HEBREWS 12:15)

FIFTH COMMAND:
HAVE COMPASSION ON SOME; MAKING A DIFFERENCE BETWEEN THOSE WHO ARE WEAK AND THOSE WHO ARE PROUD AND ARROGANT OF HEART AND UNWILLING TO OBEY TRUTH
(V. 22)

SIXTH COMMAND:
SAVE THE WILLING WITH FEAR, PULLING THEM OUT OF THE FATE OF ETERNAL HELL
(V. 23)

SEVENTH COMMAND:
HATE EVEN THE GARMENT SPOTTED BY THE FLESH
(V. 23; JAMES 1:27; EPHESIANS 5:27; HEBREWS 7:25)

"THIS IS WHAT I SAY WHEN THINGS AREN'T GOING QUITE RIGHT. WHEN OTHER PEOPLE TRY TO FRUSTRATE ME, CHALLENGE ME, OR I AM HAVING A NOT-SO-EASY TIME, I SAY 'JESUS COME TO THE MEETING." IT WORKS FOR ME!